Adventure Guide to Maine's Historic Covered Bridges

MAINE'S HISTORIC COVERED BRIDGES

Maine's Historic Covered Bridges

by Angela Quintal-Snowman

Please Note: Outdoor adventure and exploration is potentially hazardous. The publisher and author did their best to ensure accuracy of all information at the time of publication, however, they cannot accept responsibility for any loss, injury, or inconvenience experienced by anyone as a result of information or advice in this book. Also, land ownership and trails change over time. If you discover changes in ownership, trails, or any other inaccurate information please let us know so we can correct it for future editions. The author and publisher also welcome any comments or suggestions.

Contact:
Untamed Mainer
PO Box 109
Little Deer Isle, ME 04650
Untamedmainer@gmail.com
UntamedMainer.com

Table of Contents

Maine's Historic Covered Bridges

There was once 120 covered bridges throughout Maine, built between the mid-1800s and early 1900s. The bridges were constructed to help travelers and horse drawn carriages cross Maine's rivers, many of which can become raging during times of heavy rains and floods and carry anything in their path downstream. Roofs were added to the bridges to protect those crossing the rivers, to protect the bridge structure, and keep snow and ice off of the timbers.

Floods, ice, fires, redevelopment and several freshets destroyed most of Maine's 120 covered bridges. A freshet is when a river floods from melting snow and ice in the spring or heavy rains. Maine experienced several freshets that destroyed not only covered bridges but also mills, dams, and many houses, with the most notable being The Great Freshet of 1896.

Today, Maine has nine covered bridges still standing. Of those nine bridges, only seven are the original bridges that were built by Maine's original bridge builders before the early 1900's. Both Lowe's Bridge and Babb's Bridge were destroyed by a flood and fire in the past 40 years. Exact replicas of the original bridges were reconstructed in their place.

Maine's Remaining Covered Bridges:

Map Pin	Bridge Name	Location	Page Number
1	Babb's Bridge	Windham	7
2	Bennett-Bean Bridge	Wilson's Mills	9
3	Hemlock Bridge	Fryeburg	13
4	Lovejoy Bridge	Andover	24
5	Low's Bridge	Guilford/Sangerville	30
6	Porter/Parsonsfield Bridge	Porter	34
7	Robyville Bridge	Corinth	37
8	Sunday River/Artist's Bridge	Newry	41
9	Watson Bridge	Littleton	44

Maine Covered Bridge Truss Types

Below are the typical truss types used to build the covered bridges that are still standing in Maine. Some trusses are a combination of several types, such as Paddleford with an Arch for additional support.

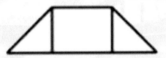

Queen Post

Queen Post trusses span long openings and use two supporting posts.

Long

Long trusses have 3 wood diagonals and double timber posts in each panel.

Paddleford

Paddleford trusses have counterbraces at the ends which cross both the kingposts and the chords. Inside arches (right) are often added.

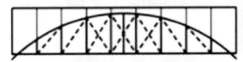

Arch

Arches can be tied (above) or hinged. The ends of hinged arches sit on the face of the abutments. Suspension types differ and include verticals, diagonals, and crossed X bracing.

Howe (usual)

Usual Howe trusses have three wood diagonals with 2-3 vertical iron rods (dashed lines).

Howe (single)

Single Howe trusses have single wood diagonals with single vertical iron rods (dashed lines).

MAINE'S HISTORIC COVERED BRIDGES

Locations of Maine's Historic Covered Bridges

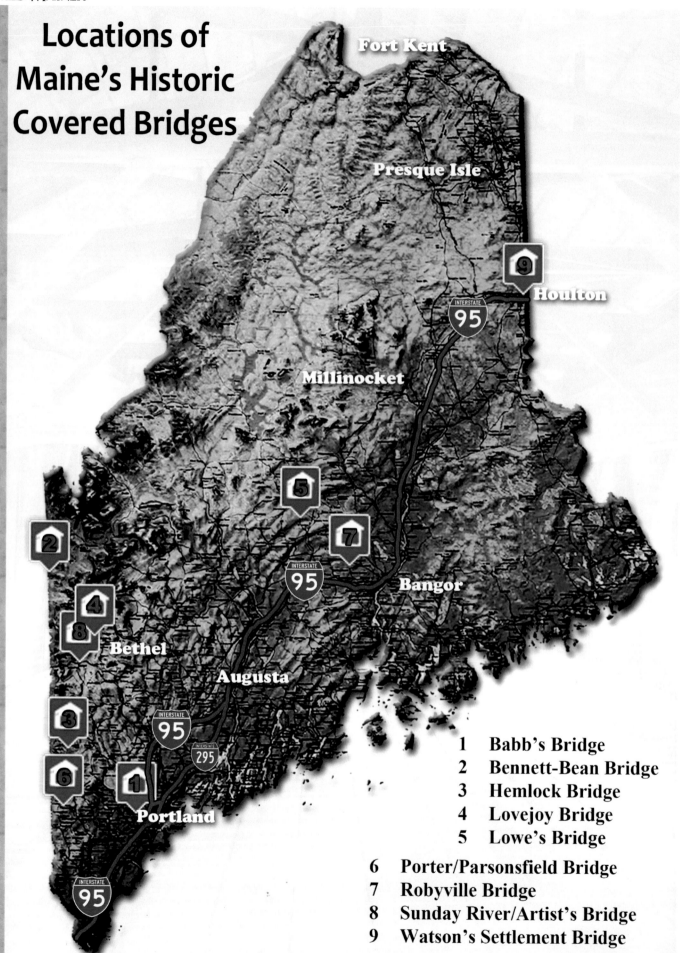

1. Babb's Bridge
2. Bennett-Bean Bridge
3. Hemlock Bridge
4. Lovejoy Bridge
5. Lowe's Bridge

6. Porter/Parsonsfield Bridge
7. Robyville Bridge
8. Sunday River/Artist's Bridge
9. Watson's Settlement Bridge

MAINE'S HISTORIC COVERED BRIDGES

Babb's Bridge

Babb's Bridge

Location: Hurricane Road, Windham/Gorham
Lat./Long: 43.766042 N, -70.4479193 W
DeLorme: Map 5, D2
Built: 1840, 1976
Length: 79'
Truss Type: Queenpost
Water: Presumpscot River
About: Named after the Babb family who lived nearby, Babb's Bridge, originally build in 1840, was Maine's oldest covered bridge. Vandals burned the original bridge in 1973, and Maine DOT reconstructed an exact replica of the bridge using locally milled lumber. The bridge spans the Presumpscot River and connects the towns of Windham and Gorham.

Babb's Bridge

NOTES: Babb's Bridge is located on a quiet backroad on the Windham/Gorham line. There is space to park before and after the bridge. The Presumpscot River the bridge spans is very clean and clear. This bridge is still in use and you can drive over it.

② Bennett-Bean Bridge

Bennett-Bean Bridge

Location: Littlehale Road, Wilson's Mills/Lincoln Plantation

Lat./Long: 44.919128 N, -71.03840 W

DeLorme: Map 27, E5

Built: 1898-1901

Length: 93'

Truss Type: Paddleford

Water: Magalloway River

About: Construction was under way in 1898 when the abutments were completed. Bethel bridge construction company Mason Brothers completed the bridge in 1901. (**Note:** Google Maps has the river incorrectly labeled as *Bear Brook* instead of *Magalloway River*).

2 Bennett-Bean Bridge

② Bennett-Bean Bridge

NOTES: The road to the Bennett-Bean covered bridge passes through a small campground (see below). You may drive down the short dirt road (through the campground) to view and photograph the bridge, but please be respectful of those camping and the landowner. Park off to the side on the dirt road but not in the grass. The Bennett-Bean bridge is closed to vehicles but you can walk through it. As you can see in the first photo, there is a beautiful mountain just behind the bridge, perfect for scenic shots. Head towards Rangeley and follow Route 4 on your way back home if you can. The views on that section of the road are incredible anytime of year!

Bennett-Bean
Covered Bridge
Location

② Bennett-Bean Bridge

⬢ Hemlock Bridge

Hemlock Bridge

Location: Hemlock Bridge Road, Fryeburg
Lat./Long: 44.079523 N, -70.90308 W
DeLorme: Map 4, A2
Built: 1857
Length: 109'
Truss Type: Paddleford with arch
Water: Old Course Saco River
About: This covered bridge was built on granite abutments to prevent it from being washed away in high water. The trusses were strengthened with laminated wood arches. In 1988 it was reinforced to carry vehicle traffic. In 2002 the American Society of Civil Engineers designated Hemlock Bridge a Maine Historic Civil Engineering Landmark.

Hemlock Bridge

NOTES: Hemlock Bridge is the hidden gem of Maine's covered bridges. This was by far my favorite bridge to visit, mainly because of it's location. The road to this bridge is a dirt road, and it feels like a very long drive when you're dodging potholes for the last 3 miles. Despite the potholes, it's certainly worth the drive (although maybe not during mud season!). This bridge can be driven over and has a fantastic parking area in a pine grove. There is plenty of space to have a picnic or just relax next to the river. I love to paddle, and looking at the Old Course Saco River below the bridge and the

Hemlock Bridge

beautiful boat launch leading into the crystal clear waters made me want to go home, grab my canoe and explore what's beyond the river bend! It didn't help that I saw a guy packing up his canoe and heading out as I arrived! The scenery heading towards and away from the bridge is also incredible. You pass through a farmland with mountain views and follow the river for a bit until you reach Frog Alley. While it may be a bit out of the way, you won't regret checking out this covered bridge. Any type of car should be able to make the trek, as long as you drive careful and slow. If your car doesn't have much clearance or gets stuck easy, you may want to wait until after mud season.

15

Hemlock Bridge

Hemlock Bridge

[4] Lovejoy Bridge

Lovejoy Bridge

Location: Covered Bridge Road, Andover
Lat./Long: 44.593341 N, -70.73337 W
DeLorme: Map 18, D4
Built: 1868
Length: 70'
Truss Type: Paddleford
Water: Ellis River
About: The Lovejoy Bridge is Maine's shortest covered bridge, spanning just 70 feet. The bridge was named after a nearby family who lived on the eastern side of the river. High waters in 1936 almost cost two curious boys their lives at the bridge. The boys paddled their canoe up next to the bridge. The river was just a few inches lower than the bottom of the bridge that day. They hoped to float next to the bridge but the strong current tipped their canoe. At the same time a Registered Maine Guide was canoeing the river and rescued the boys. In 1983 another incident almost cost a sand truck driver his life when the truck fell through the bridge deck. This prompted reinforcement in 1984 to support traffic.

🔷④ Lovejoy Bridge

NOTES: I visited the Lovejoy covered bridge last winter and again this summer, as you will notice in the photos. It is relatively close to the Sunday River/Artist's Covered Bridge and is worth the drive! This bridge is located on a side road off the main road and there is space to park on either side of the bridge. You can drive over the bridge and the roads leading to and from the bridge pass through incredible countryside. The views from the bridge are beautiful, including a distant mountain and the crystal clear river below. The banks of the river are also very beautiful with a large sand bar on one side.

4 Lovejoy Bridge

④ Lovejoy Bridge

4 Lovejoy Bridge

Ⓢ Low's Bridge

Low's Bridge

Location: Covered Bridge Road, Guilford/Sangerville
Lat./Long: 45.175196 N, -69.31511 W
DeLorme: Map 32, B1
Built: 1830, 1990
Length: 120'
Truss Type: Paddleford
Water: Piscataquis River
About: Low's Bridge was originally built in 1830 but washed away in flood waters April 1st, 1987. In 1990 another bridge was build on the original abutments patterened after the original design. The new bridge was upgraded to hold more weight and was raised up to prevent future flooding. The bridge spans the Piscataquis River, just off Route 15, and connects the towns of Guilford and Sangerville. The bridge is also spelled Lowe's in some locations

⑤ Low's Bridge

NOTES: I visited Low's bridge last winter. The bridge is a beautiful replica of the original, and is open to vehicle traffic in the summer and snowmobiles in the winter. The road on the other side is a dirt road and becomes a dead end. It was very cool to watch snowmobiles cruise through a covered bridge! Check out my covered bridge video on my YouTube channel to see for yourself!

5 Low's Bridge

Porter - Parsonsfield Bridge

Location: 13N Road, Porter
Lat./Long: 43.791001 N, -70.93795 W
DeLorme: Map 4, D1
Built: 1859
Length: 152'
Truss Type: Paddleford
Water: Ossipee River
About: A joint building effort between the towns of Porter and Parsonsfield gave the bridge its name. Eventually there was a dispute between the two towns over building and maintaining the new bridge. Selectmen from each town met at the bridge and the dispute continued until a selectman from Parsonsfield tossed his jackknife at the middle of the bridge and proclaimed "The town of Parsonsfield shall build so far and no further!" Eventually laminated wooden arches were added to the span for strength, although the bridge is closed to traffic today.

Porter - Parsonsfield Bridge

NOTES: Apparently the towns continued to dispute over the bridge. As you will notice when you visit, on one end of the bridge the sign reads "Porter-Parsonsfield Bridge" and on the other end of the bridge it reads "Parsonsfield-Porter Bridge." I'm sure you can guess which side each one goes on! You will see the bridge as you cross the river on the new bridge. This bridge is closed to vehicle traffic, but you can walk across it. If you follow your GPS it may direct you to take the left turn before the new bridge. This appears to be a private drive so I didn't bother to check it out. Instead, I drove over the new bridge and turned down a short dirt road into a large parking lot.

Porter - Parsonsfield Bridge

MAINE'S HISTORIC COVERED BRIDGES

⑦ Robyville Bridge

Robyville Bridge

Location: Covered Bridge Road, Corinth
Lat./Long: 44.943387 N, -68.96858 W
DeLorme: Map 32, E5
Built: 1876
Length: 73'
Truss Type: Howe, Long Truss
Water: Kenduskeag Stream
About: The Robyville Bridge is the only bridge in Maine that is completely shingle-covered. Reinforcements were added to the bridge in 1984 to support automobile traffic. In 2002 the bridge was designated a Maine Historic Engineering Landmark because it is the oldest surviving example of a Long Truss system used in a Maine covered bridge.

7 Robyville Bridge

HORSES AND MULES AT A WALK
OR 1 DOLLAR FINE
NO SPITTING – NO SEEGARS

NOTES: I visited the Robyville covered bridge last winter as well. This bridge is located on a rural road that doesn't have a lot of traffic. The bridge can be driven over, and there is a fantastic spot beside the river with picnic tables to have lunch. Remember no spitting or seegars when crossing the bridge on foot, and no horse or mule races.

⑦ Robyville Bridge

7 Robyville Bridge

Sunday River/Artist's Bridge

Sunday River Bridge
(Artist's Covered Bridge)

Location: Sunday River Road, Newry
Lat./Long: 44.492365 N, -70.84338 W
DeLorme: Map 10 A2
Built: 1872
Length: 87'
Truss Type: Paddleford
Water: Sunday River
About: This bridge is often referred to as the Artist's Bridge, although the source of the name is debatable. Some say the name comes from the fact that the bridge is the most photographed and painted bridge in the state. Others claim it comes from the fact that artist John Enncking spent so much time painting at the bridge during his stay with a local family, the family began referring to it as the Artist's Bridge. The bridge was in use until 1958, when a new, stronger bridge was built for automobile traffic.

⑧ Sunday River/Artist's Bridge

NOTES: Be warned about the Sunday River covered bridge: It is hard to get a photo of the bridge without someone on it during foliage season because so many other people are there! It can be challenging to get a parking spot as well. This very popular bridge is no longer open to traffic but you can walk across it. The river below is beautiful and the landscape is amazing.

8 Sunday River/Artist's Bridge

Watson's Bridge

Watson's Bridge

Location: Framingham Road, Littleton
Lat./Long: 46.209867,-67.80010
DeLorme: Map 59 E4
Built: 1911
Length: 170'
Truss Type: Howe
Water: Meduxnekeag Stream
About: This covered bridge was named after the nearby Watson homestead. It is the most northern and youngest of all of Maine's covered bridges. The bridge has two spans for a total of 170 feet over the Meduxnekeag Stream. When a new bridge was built in 1984, Watson's Bridge was closed to automobile traffic.

Watson Bridge

NOTES: The bridge was originally named Watson Bridge and locals still call it that, although the D.O.T. refers to the bridge as the Watson Settlement Bridge (along with the American Society of Civil Engineers). Not far from the bridge is the original Watson Settlement and the Canadian border. Watson Bridge is definitely one of the most "colorful" of all the bridges with an extensive amount of graffiti on the inside. The bridge is still beautiful and worth the trip up north. While you're in Houlton stop downtown to check out the Gateway Bridge (footbridge) and take a drive to the only place in America where you can be on Route 1 and Route 2 at the same time!

Watson Bridge

Maine's Covered Bridges Day Trip

Enjoy incredible scenery and a nice drive through the country- Visit 6 covered bridges in one day! Drive through farmlands and forests, pass by mountains and cross beautiful rivers on this fantastic scenic drive. Below are turn-by-turn directions for your adventure:

Start at:
Babb's Bridge

Hurricane Rd, Gorham, ME 04038

1. Head northwest on Hurricane Rd toward Wilson Rd

0.6 mi

2. Turn left onto Wilson Rd

1.2 mi

3. Turn right onto ME-237 N

2.1 mi

4. Turn left onto ME-35 S

3.7 mi

5. Turn right onto ME-25 W

21.7 mi

6. Turn left onto ME-160 S

0.2 mi

7. Turn left
   ⓘ Destination will be on the right

0.2 mi

45 min (29.7 mi)

MAINE'S HISTORIC COVERED BRIDGES

Maine's Covered Bridges Day Trip

Porter-Parsonfield Bridge
Parsonsfield, ME 04047

↑ 8. Head north toward ME-160 S

25 s (0.2 mi)

Continue on ME-160 N to Brownfield

23 min (15.3 mi)

↱ 9. Turn right onto ME-160 N

0.2 mi

↱ 10. Turn right onto ME-160 N/ME-25 E

2.6 mi

↰ 11. Turn left onto ME-160 N

0.1 mi

↱ 12. Turn right to stay on ME-160 N

0.6 mi

↰ 13. Turn left to stay on ME-160 N

9.4 mi

↱ 14. Turn right onto Pig St

0.9 mi

↰ 15. Turn left onto ME-113 N/ME-5 N

184 ft

↱ 16. Turn right onto ME-160 N

1.5 mi

Continue on Lords Hill Rd. Take W Denmark Rd and Hemlock Bridge Rd to Frog Alley in Fryeburg

20 min (9.1 mi)

↑ 17. Continue straight onto Lords Hill Rd

1.7 mi

↰ 18. Turn left onto Rocky Knoll Rd

0.4 mi

↱ 19. Turn right onto Walkers Falls Rd

0.1 mi

↑ 20. Walkers Falls Rd turns right and becomes Firelane 77

0.2 mi

↰ 21. Slight left onto Fire Ln 84/Smith Rd

0.7 mi

↱ 22. Turn right onto W Denmark Rd/Rocky Knoll Rd

0.6 mi

↰ 23. Turn left onto Denmark Rd

2.4 mi

↑ 24. Continue onto Hemlock Bridge Rd

2.9 mi

Maine's Covered Bridges Day Trip

↑   25.   Continue onto Frog Alley

299 ft

43 min (24.6 mi)

Hemlock Bridge
East Fryeburg, Fryeburg, ME 04037

↑   26.   Head southwest on Frog Alley

1.1 mi

↱   27.   Turn right to stay on Frog Alley

0.9 mi

↱   28.   Turn right onto ME-5 N

16.9 mi

↰   29.   Turn left onto ME-35 N/ME-5 N

12.7 mi

↱   30.   Turn right onto US-2 F ## Lovejoy Bridge
Andover, ME 04216

↰   31.   Turn left onto Sunday
    ⓘ Destination will be (↑   37.   Head west on Covered Bridge Rd toward ME-5 S

56 min (38.5 mi)

Sunday River Bridge
Sunday River, Newry, ME 04261

↑   32.   Head south on Sunday River Rd toward Monkey Brook Rd

3.3 mi

↰   33.   Turn left onto Martin Ln

0.3 mi

↰   34.   Turn left onto US-2 E

8.7 mi

↰   35.   Turn left onto ME-5 N

7.6 mi

↱   36.   Turn right onto Covered Bridge Rd

0.2 mi

26 min (20.1 mi)

Maine's Covered Bridges Day Trip

Lovejoy Bridge
Andover, ME 04216

↑ 37. Head west on Covered Bridge Rd toward ME-5 S

30 s (0.2 mi)

↱ 38. Turn right onto ME-5 N

5 min (3.1 mi)

Follow Upton Rd and Andover Rd to ME-26 N in Upton

26 min (14.0 mi)

↰ 39. Turn left onto Newton St

0.3 mi

↑ 40. Newton St turns slightly right and becomes Upton Rd

5.0 mi

↑ 41. Continue onto Andover Rd

8.8 mi

Take NH-26 W and NH-16 N to Littlehale Rd in Lincoln

33 min (23.3 mi)

↗ 42. Slight right onto ME-26 N
   ℹ Entering New Hampshire

1.8 mi

↑ 43. Continue onto NH-26 W

8.3 mi

↱ 44. Turn right onto NH-16 N
   ℹ Entering Maine

8.9 mi

↑ 45. Continue onto ME-16 E

4.4 mi

↰ 46. Turn left onto Littlehale Rd
   ⚠ May be closed at certain times or days

1 min (0.3 mi)

1 h 6 min (40.8 mi)

Bennett Bridge
Errol, ME 03579

Please Help Keep
Maine's Wilderness Untamed!

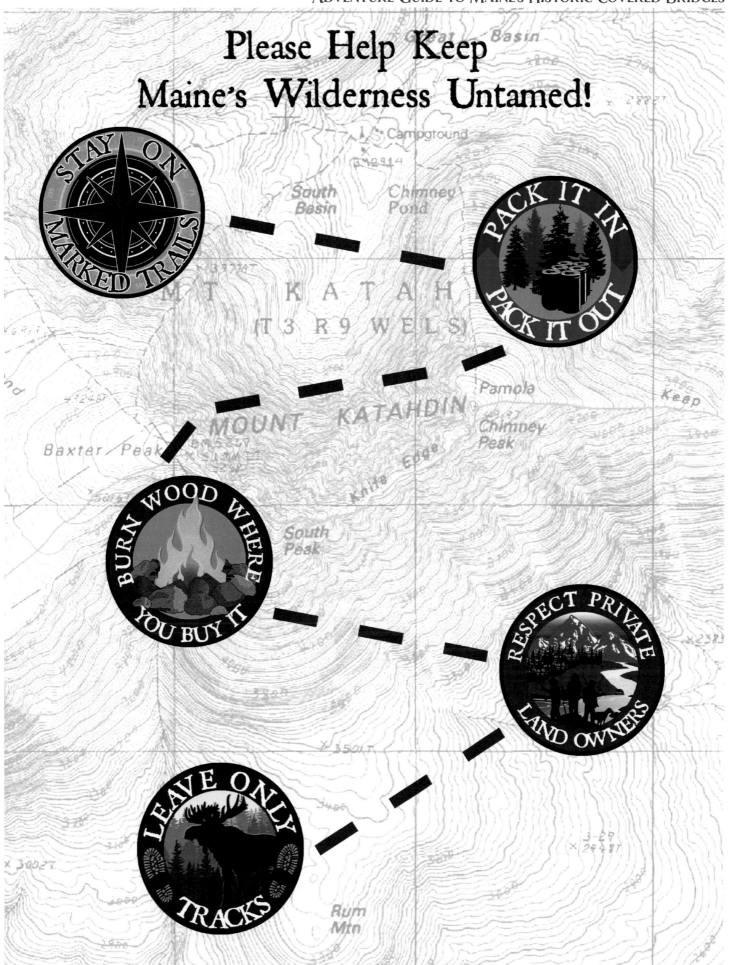